# Chocolate Dreams

POEMS BY ARNOLD ADOFF

# Chocolate Dreams

ILLUSTRATED BY TURI MacCOMBIE

LOTHROP, LEE & SHEPARD BOOKS    NEW YORK

First Edition 1 2 3 4 5 6 7 8 9 10

Library of Congress Cataloging in Publication Data
Adoff, Arnold. Chocolate dreams.
Summary: Original poems on a favorite subject by a chocolate lover. 1. Children's
poetry, American. 2. Chocolate—Juvenile poetry. [1.Chocolate—Poetry.
2. American poetry] I. MacCombie, Turi, ill. II. Title.
PS3551.D66C49 1989 811'.54 88-27208
ISBN 0-688-06822-7 ISBN 0-688-06823-5 (lib. bdg.)

**Inspiration: Chocolate**

Chocolate
 I
Love
   You So
       I
Want
   To
Marry
   You
   And
Live
   Forever
       In The
       Flavor
Of Your
   Brown

Dedication: To Loving Family And Friends,
Editors And Artists: All Who
Feed Me Chocolate Kisses Hugs
                And
Smiles  B e y o n d  Any  Flavor.

**Dear Reader:**

We will be watching very lovingly to make sure that no one licks any of these pages, bites the binding, or chews the covers of this chocolate book.

Once you have finished some sweet pieces, get up and go to some room or store. Visit very full refrigerators. Get something c h o c o l a t e to stuff in your mouth. Then come back to this book and read some more. The best way to read this writing is by biting and chewing in unison (all together now) with these delicious words.

Please do not drip any chocolate juice from your mouth onto these pages. Please do not lick these pages, bite the binding, or chew the covers of this chocolate book. Just laugh and look and be hungry always for that chocolate love so sweet and pure.

Now taste these happy chocolate dreams.

**Chocolate Dreams. One.**

Awake   I'll   Walk.
         I'll   Run.
         I'll Crawl.
         I'll Creep.
         I'll   Bake
         A Simple
         Chocolate
         Cake.

Alseep   I'll   Bite.
         I'll   Eat.
         I'll   Lick.
         I'll   Drip.
         I'll Chew.
         I'll   Heat
         A Simple
         Pot
         Of
         Hot
         Chocolate
         Stew.

**Chocolate Dreams. Two.**

Chocolate Sun.
Chocolate Moon.
Chocolate Clouds.
Chocolate Raindrops.
Chocolate Sprinkles   On
                      My
Chocolate Head.

Chocolate   Hair.
Chocolate   Face.
Chocolate   Body.
Chocolate   Bed.
Chocolate Squishing   In
                      My
Chocolate Boots  As I
                      Run
                   Through
Chocolate Streets    And
                    Splash
                   Through
Chocolate Puddles   And
                     Wade
                    Across
Chocolate Streams. I
                     Must
                     Swim
                     Swift
Chocolate Rivers.   I
                     Must
                     Swim
                     Some
                 Unsweetened
Chocolate Sea.      I
                  Dream A
Chocolate World     For
                     Me.

Chocolate World     For
                     Me.

**Chocolate Dreams   And   Chocolate Schemes**

keep popping  in my head.
In  some  sweet  morning
English  class    I  cook
my  parts    of  chocolate
                                dreams
     instead        of
     looking      at   the  parts
                          of speech
that uncooked
words   become   in   my
                                  sweet
t e a c h e r ' s        recipes.


While nodding  on my bed
on  homework  afternoons,
I   scheme
     scheme  my
for chocolate     s a l a d
at    the table      tonight.
Macaroni
and chocolate in a steaming pan will be
the main course of my  chocolate dinner
plan, if I am right about  the menu  in
                        the kitchen down below.

I  k n o w   d e s s e r t   i s   b r o w n.

## Those Who Do Not Study History Are Doomed.

It is so hard   to read about   the glories
of growing   cotton   in the   ante   bellum
South, when my Northern teeth sit idle in
my   c o n t e m p o r a r y   empty   mouth.

The past was last night's   double   fudge
                    d e l i g h t
and I can almost taste the p r e s e n t
as my chocolate bar melts under a   fading
                    S o u t h e r n   s u n.


## In This Last Class   Before Lunch, I Close My Eyes

and think I feel the   unreal yet palpable crunch
of a chocolate-covered   fancy-foiled
decidedly  uncafeterial confection
between  my masticating  molars.
I can taste   the sweet
                    choco late,
          warm
as it melts
against the palate of my up p er
                    m o u t h
to coat and slide right down  my
                    t h r o a t.
I bring a real hunger  for learning
to this last class   before lunch. I close my eyes.

**Three-Thirty**

every afternoon    during school days
I make it through   the front door
and head straight   into the kitchen
for a glass. As I pour and drink to
pour again   I raise   my hand   in
mock salute   and gently (but firmly)
shake the last track of liquid down
the side of the glass   and onto   my
w a i t i n g          t o n g u e.

I think of my teacher   Mrs. McNasty
and her daily yell   her daily frown
her daily quiz   the f i n a l bell
that p r o p e l s me home each day
to drink and to forget.
L i s t e n        champs:
It's chocolate milk time
for this young American
and I must go   for all
the  g u s t o
                    I can get.

## The Rain Falling On West Train Tracks, Ohio,

never seems to stop until it turns to snow
with winter cold. This is a new town for us,
with a new wet weather for my most unhappy
sinuses. But there is this girl  in my class
at Power Mouse  Junior High School  whose
hair is the color of the best European candy
featured in the library magazines. And   the
                                        sun,
which is always and exclusively s h i n ing
over her sweet head, has  m e l t e d  some
of that fine brown down, to drip   sprinkled
                                        drops

of choc
        o
        late  freckles  <sup>on</sup><sub>to</sub>  her  shining  cheeks.

15

**I Meet   Sweet Sue   For A Walk**
**On A Cold And Sunny Afternoon.**

The sky is so blue after last night
and  this  morning   of  hard  snowing.  I  think
that the sky is as blue as Sue's eyes.
Or her eyes are as blue as the sky.
The village trucks have plowed a path
into the high snow, and we seem to walk
some bright  white  tunnel  through
a  foreign  land.  But  this  is  our  same  street
we  always  w a l k  h o l d i n g  h a n d s.

This is a walk for hot chocolate  on a cold day.
This is a walk for hot brown
                              chocolate
on a cold w h i t e day.

In our favorite restaurant,  Susan sits down
at our favorite table   with a steaming cup.
Two melting marshmallows try to stay floating
on the hot brown top.  Steam rises. Susan sips.
I
stop staring at blue eyes   and brown cups
              and dive into the  hot  tub  of
                                  hot
          c h o c o l a t e
in  the  center  of  this  hot  chocolate  shop.

I swim  and drink  and  float
          and drink  and   dive
          and drink  and drink
          and drink  and I  am
a melting marshmallow in the hot tub
of my bubbling  choc o late l o v e.

I wave to blue-eyed Susan  who throws me
  a d o u g h n u t  instead of a towel.

16

## I Will Hold  Your Hand

and take   a fine    walk
around    the lake   with
you.
I will hold   your hand
and  sit down at    the
side
walk
café   to share  a piece
of lemon cake   or two.
I  will hold   your hand
and eat   some  popcorn
as  we    stroll    around
the zoo   and see   what
we can see.  But  you
know, baby love, my own
sweet  dear  and   lovely
you:
I'm saving   all   of my
chocolate  kisses    just
for
me.

### On This Winter    After Noon,

we  are  walking
along  the  cold  s t r e e t.
Those  f i r s t
      s m i l e s
have  warmed  my
face      and your
            e y e s
burn  h o l e s
through  this  new
            and
very    expensive  down parka.
On  your  mouth
you  make  t h e
chocolate      kiss
that    melts    my
ch o c o la te  h e a r t.
Silver      flashes
in  the  winter  s u n.

## In The Moments Of Our Cookies

shared on the Zenia Avenue bench,
there are chewing sounds and our
crumb thoughts,  c r u m b  words;

and choking laughs at OldManStan
                              walking his twin,
                                        his        dog,
under  the  chocolate  chip s k y.

Only your eyes are            b i g g e r,
                                      b rowne r,
            your mouth          s w e e t e r
than
   any
chip
   can
taste.

**I Believe  In The Theory**
**That Says We Were Visited**
**Long Ago**

by spaceships full of extraterrestrial space
travelers who drew massive diagrams on the
floors of mountain plateaus; who scratched
their drawings on the walls of caves.

I'm sure they came to educate as well as
to explore. Maybe they w a n t e d to test us:
the human species inhabiting this planet.

And I think they left us with some of the
possibilities for  good  and/or  evil  that
we have to face in our perilous time: positive
use of atomic energy/nuclear destruction; the
various and lovely kinds of peanut butter/the
cosmic recipe for sad calves' liver and onions;
the marvelous, mystical, magical secret of the
cacao bean and its derivatives, byproducts,
and manufactured c o m b i n a t i o n s,
permutations, even i m i t a t i o n s/vanilla.

I believe  in the theory
that says we were visited
long ago
and, of course, I chew my chocolate in the
cause of i n t e r p l a n e t a r y peace.
I shove that sweet stuff in, and search
the heavens far above my chewing face, and
increase  u n i v e r s a l  understanding
as I f i l l my i n n e r  s  p  a  c  e .

### You Are Walking Along Eating

an excellent chocolate chip
cookie on a country road   and
                                    the
e x t r a t e r r e s t r i a l s
                          w a v e
their antennae as you pass their
                    chocolate way.
The Pod People
are rolling s l o w l y
into their   brown   pods          and
                                    great
                                    brown
                                    birds
follow along behind your
                                    falling
                                    crumbs.
You are here
on this chocolate road   with   an
excellent   chocolate   chip   cookie,
and all the creatures of a quiet
chocolate afternoon admire   your
          g o o d   t a s t e.

### In My Horror Fantasy Chiller:

I have to fight   fierce dragons;
swim through  a lake of fire  in
my  underwear; bite off the ears
of *Cujo* dogs, and send them  yelping
back to  Stephen King; hitch a  ride
with  extraterrestrials   wearing   ski
masks  in July; and   run   faster   than   rolling
boulders, Rolling Stones, and  the  hands  of  time.

When  I  arrive,  I  find  that   all   the  sweet  milk
chocolate–coated cherries  have been devoured by
my  little  brother.  He  has  been  sent  by  the  devil
from the nether regions of *Hell* (where no
chocolate  could  remain   even  a  little  unmelted)
to deprive me of my natural rights,  and  to drive
me into a  life  of  crime.

After my tears dry, I go out and mug Willy
                                        Wonka
for a bag of chocolate lollypops
(on those  nice safe  cardboard sticks).   It
                                                    is
only a matter of time  before I am caught,
tried, c o n v i c t e d, and sent to the
                                        dentist
for five-to-ten (cav i ties).

### Why I Always Brush

My dentist works in a hard hat
and a sweat band on each wrist
He uses a jackhammer drill   and
                                    his
diploma says  he is a
                    g r a d u a t e
                              of
                              the
Ohio State Highway Department
School Of Concrete Reconstruction.

He makes house calls.

## Friday The Thirteenth.

On my way to the store
I walk  under a ladder
and a   dish of vanilla
ice cream  lands on my
                 head.
Maple  walnuts  are  fall
                      ing

from   the   sky
and  I  s l i p
on        cherries
as    I    try to
run   through a
whipped  cream
sundae  dream.  On the
                    radio
they   are   saying  that
straw  berry  feels  for
                      ever
and for ever
and for ever.

I have never been more
          a f r a i d.

### I Could Never Convince Any Of The Other Members

of my family that: supermarket mice    ate holes
in the bags of  c h o c o -
l a t e-covered  r a i  sins;
the girl at the c h e c kout
counter    forgot    to pack the
package of chocolate    chunks
in our bag of g r o c eries;
when we finally arrive home
and press that z a p p er to
automatically o p e n  o u r
garage door; a l l chocolate
automatically              vaporizes
beyond the atmosphere of our
                    p l a n e t.

They say I am full
of em p ty excuses.
I  know  I am full.

### I Don't Mean To Say I Am Martian, Morkian,

or one   of the   original        Klingon
                                   K i d s .

My skin is almost never green.
My ears are   usually   round.
My friends
         are   just themselves,
                  not elves.
But   I   have
      the
p  o  w  e  r  to feel vibrations
                  emanating f r o m
                  b a g s of candy hidden
                  behind old pots and unused
                  roasting pans in the   back
                        of the   back
                  of kitchen cabinet shelves.
Once
I found  a  pound  of  the  best  chocolate-
                        c o v e r e d
almonds cleverly d i s g u i s e d as
a        can      of       dog      food.

**Chips. One.**

More Than  Two Hundred
And Forty  Million     In
                        di
                        vid
                        u
                        al
Pieces Of
Chocolate    Are    Sold
In  This   C o u n t r y
          E v e r y  D a y.

**Chips. Two.**

Malvales. The Mallow Order. A Small Order.
Malvales. The Mallow Order  Of  Flowering
Plants  In  Class  Dicotyledoneae.  There  are
                        Nine
                        F a m i l i e s
Of 3,000
      Species
Of
Plants.
They Grow Throughout The World,
Except  In  The    Arctic    Regions.

**Chips. Three.**

Theobroma Cacao. The Source Of Chocolate.
Part Of The Sterculiaceae Family.      One Of
Twenty-Two Species In This Genus.
Native From Central Amazon River
Basin And Guyana In South
America, North And West
                                                    To
Southern  M e x i c o.

Fruit Of Theobroma Cacao Is Source
Of C h o c o l a t e , Cocoa, and
                                                    Cocoa
                                                            Butter.

Cacao Contains The  Alkaloid
                            Theobromine.
                            Theobromine
Is A Greek
Word Meaning: Food Of The
                            Gods.

**The Old Math. One.**

If a train leaves Union Station,
in Chicago, at eight in the morning
carrying three thousand dozen gross of dark
almond bark and travels the average speed
of fifty-seven miles per hour for one
day, then c o l l i d e s  with a train
that left San Francisco one day
earlier  full of fifteen hundred dozen
bite-sized chocolate puppies,
how many days  will the residents
of Left Foothills, Colorado, have to
spend in the  high school gym
while the National Guard, the
Environmental Protection Agency,
and the local sheriff's department
remove the worst bite-sized bark bits
(or the worst bark-sized bite bits)
and return the area to its former
h a b i t a b l e   c o n d i t i o n ?

**The Old Math. Two.**

This box contains
eight (8) individually
wrapped
    one (1) ounce blocks
of pure dark chocolate:
which equals
five (5) school day
afternoons,
    two (2) weekend late
    night s n a c k s ,
                    and
    one (1) instant
            present        to
                        my
                        self
right now   because   it
                        is
                        still
            raining.

I  love  to  sub  tr  act.


**Mathematical Metric Conversion Version.**

Eight ounces of all natural, semi-
    sweet chocolate treats: is
    equal to two-hundred-a n d-
    twenty-six-point-eight grams
            of all natural, semi-
    sweet chocolate treats: is
    equal to the biggest        belly
                            ache
        this
        side   of the   At    lan   tic.

### I Raise My Voice Most High, This Night,

in praise of *Milk Duds*®: most improbably
named candy in its yellow box; m o s t
wonderfully delicious candy in its most
yellow box; most deliciously wonderful
chocolate-covered candy spheres within
yellow boxes.
Through permanently clenched t e e t h
I raise my voice most high, this night,
to praise and g u r g l e out three
c a r a m e l i c c h e e r s.

In the last row of the Cine I-II-III-Infinity,
at the beginning of the last l a t e show on a
Saturday night in West Fish Float, California,
I stuff my mouth with *Milk Duds*® and experience
an all-too-rare moment of postpubescent peace
with my a g e r a c e gender and country of
                                    o r i g i n .

**Let The Biter Beware.**

In the   center   of each
                pale
                milk
c h o c o l a t e  lump
there is a  hard    nut
waiting  to bump  your
front  tooth  into  the
d e n t i s t's  chair.

In the   center   of each
                dark
                deep
c h o c o l a t e  hunk
there  is  a  car a mel
chunk   just waiting  to
                glue
your   teeth  to geth er
            for   ev   er.

T a k e
c a r e.

34

**T w o  A M**

and I am standing on this cold kitchen floor.
There are always reasons  in the middle of
the night.  I had to go to the bathroom.
          I had a bad dream about flying
          fudge brownies attacking
                    Mr. & Mrs.
                    Betterbar.
I woke up remembering  that I had forgotten
to brush my teeth  before I went to bed.   Or
there could be a very important Italian
                         soccer     game
unfolding (and unviewed by me) on the
international  dish-antennaed  television
                              cable
I am able to click into life on my t u b e.

But there is a chocolate-covered d o u b l e
chocolate  ice  cream  bar  lying  a l o n e
on  the  lower  left-hand  shelf  of  the  freezer.
I  know  it  is  there.  I  know  it  is  still  there.
I also know it has my name printed  imprinted
                              embossed
                              engraved
i n t o   i t s   i c e   s l i c k   s t i c k.

### Why Did The Fireman

wear red suspenders: to get to the
other side of the candy store. Why
did the chicken cross the road: to
h o l d  u p  her  p a n t s. Why
did the chocolate bunny get hit by
   the chocolate car: because its
      chocolate  ear
        had  been  bitten  off  the
                  evening
                  before,
  so it couldn't hear
  the chocolate horn, a n d  its
              suspenders
had melted  in the  morning  sun,
and it did  not look b o t h  ways
out of its  m a r s h  m a l l o w
                e y e s.

**Life In The Forest.**
**Or: Bad News...**
                  **Good News...**
    **Bad News....**

First: Hansel and Gretel try to follow
a trail of chocolate chips and chocolate-
covered raisins back to their home.
But the sun melts the chips, and the tiny
pools of chocolate are licked up by
chocolate chip–loving chipmunks. And the
raisins are pecked up by the birds
who usually eat boring bread crumbs in
                                    this
                                 story.

So they become hopelessly lost
and end up at the candy house of the
wicked
witch  who captures them both.   But
                               the
wicked
witch  is so wicked that she feeds them
on a strict diet of broccoli and apple
juice, and they both become so big and
strong that they break out of their cages,
push the mean witch into an oven  full of
toasted tofu tarts, and run away back
                        home.

Upon hearing the wondrous tale of their
broccoli behavior and escape, their
parents vow to buy only broccoli and
apple juice forevermore. And Hansel
                                    and
                          Gretel
are put to work chopping wood to pay
for all this green goodness. Healthy
and tired and sad, they fall asleep
each night so hungry for a brown morsel
of mouth-melting chocolate…thinking of
the candy house in the forest…and the
kindly face
                of the
smiling
witch.

## A  N a t u r e  S t o r y .

There is a girl in West Shopping Mall, Missouri,
who saves all of her Christmas and birthday
money, and baby-sitting earnings, and empty-
bottle-deposit change from the first of the
year until after all the colored eggs have been
peeled and chopped into egg salad.
Certainly, by the end of April the last Easter
                                        Basket
has been emptied of its chocolate eggs
and chocolate-covered marshmallows
and (sighingly) solid milk chocolate bunnies,
right down to a mound of green plastic grass
                                        shreds
and assorted balls of tightly rolled
        f o i l  w r a p p i n g s .

It  is  then  that  this  girl  walks  over  to
Fiorucci and Bernstein Candy Store and
Gourmet Diner  on a certain sunny after
                                        noon
after school, her coat pockets
and purse bulging and jingling
all  d o w n  the  s t r eets.
It is then that she buys  every  one of
Mrs. Athena Suchard's (she is the new owner
of the F&B  Candy Store and Gourmet Diner)
left-over-half-price-or-less-on-sale-get-rid-
of-them-before-it-turns-hot-while-they-last-
100%-home-made-100%-pure-milk-chocolate-top-
of-the-line-solid-ohhh-sohh-s  o  l  i  d:rabbits/
                                        bunnies/
                                        rabbits:

c h o c o l a t e,
            all
    c h o c o l a t e.

And the girl carries all the surplus bargain
                                     bunnies
home in several of Mrs. Suchard's
F&B brown paper shopping bags and calmly
walks into her home in the broad daylight
of a sunny afternoon  and  heads  for  the
                                     garage.
In the right rear corner of the garage,
behind two broken lawn mowers and next
summer's patio furniture, is the large
chest-style freezer, h u m m i n g  away
in the shadowy light. She lifts the freezer
lid, stacks the chocolate rabbits a l o n g
the bottom and sides and all-the-way-up-to-
the-top of the freezer until it is full. As
                                    she
pulls the freezer lid closed, there is just
a faint smell of Easter: past  present  a n d
                                  future

in    the  garage    air.


Later that evening, as the girl and her mother
talk quietly in the family room before dinner,
they agree that the freezer space belongs to
the girl in exchange for a month of helping-
to-paint-the-back-bedrooms and d i g g i n g
up the garden.
You know, she says to her mother, I can, if I
feel like it, at any time this spring, summer,
or fall (or even next winter), go into the
garage and open the freezer and bite off the
head, or nibble on an ear, or c h e w a foot,
of my very own 100% solid milk chocolate
d e l i c i o u s rabbit. It is always rabbit
season in my life. (And I can feel better with
this chocolate help at finals time, next term,
or during cheerleader tryouts in August.
I can feel better any time. I can.)

Then the girl and her mother go out together into the garage and back to the chest-style freezer in the right rear corner, and they lift the lid of the freezer and look down in
                                                    to
the wide and high stack of beautiful solid milk chocolate rabbits so neatly set in rows before their eyes.
And the girl and her mother smile at e a c h
                                    o t h e r
with the great warm and close friendship    of
                                            two
people who know and love all the creatures of this earth, all the animals, great and
                                            small
and
one
hundred
percent
solid.

**In Public, I Pick A Piece Or Two From The Plate.**

I think people in the room are watching
my fingers as they move to my mouth.
I try to keep the delicious square or chunk
of chocolate candy in a hot suction grip
between my palate and tongue.
The chocolate melts and slips down my throat
in a thick milk chocolate (or semisweet)
trickle   or drip   at once warm and cool,
sweet and thick, and  f a i n t l y  reminding
some part of my  oldest  memory  of thousands
of years ago in a rich green rain forest under
                                        broadest
                                             leaves.
Even while smiling, my lips  s t a y   s h u t,
                              s t a y   c l o sed.


In private, I use all of the fingers of my right
                                             hand
and the palm  and the heel of the hand
to grab a handful of chocolate candies
from the plate. I place them in my mouth
                              in
                                   to my mouth
in multiples  together,
as if they would be lonely  going in only
one at a time.
I eat fast. I  love  most  the combining
and mingling of various flavors  melting
and mixing in my mouth at the same time:
orange bittersweet,   cherry milk
chocolate, raspberry cream delights. S o m e
                                   t i m e s
some chocolate juice will drip
and dribble out  of the corner
of my mouth, w h i l e I smile
my  s h y  brown  s m i l e.

## The Straw

was invented by Sweet Irving Chaulkstein-Jones,
who fell into a vat of chocolate milk one day
while stirring. As he came up for the first
time, he grabbed a sheet of paper from the
counter. (You need to have a counter to count
how many times you go down and come up.) When
he came up for the second time, he rolled the
paper tightly into a long narrow tube and
stuck it in his mouth and proceeded to call
for help. But not much sound comes out of a
long thin tube of paper stuck in a yelling
mouth submerged under chocolate milk. When he
came up for the third time, he began to drink
and suck and slurp and swizzle the chocolate
milk all around him through the rolled-up
tube of paper and into his Chaulkstein-Jones
stomach. In a little while the vat was empty,
Irving's stomach was full, his life had been
saved, and the straw was invented for all time.

However, poor unlucky Irving Chaulkstein-Jones
never lived long enough to enjoy any of the
fame and/or fortune from his most brilliant
invention. The following week he fell into the
chocolate milk carton–making machine and
ended up in Peoria and Los Angeles and Tulsa
and Toronto and in the refrigerated showcase
of a fine new Kroger's in Milk
                                    wau
                                    kee, W i s c o n sin.

**L a b e l s : O n e :**

Sugar, Wheat Flour, Vegetable Oil Shortening, Milk Chocolate (23%), Cocoa Powder, Milk Powder,

Malt, Caramel, E150, Artificial Vanilla Flavor.

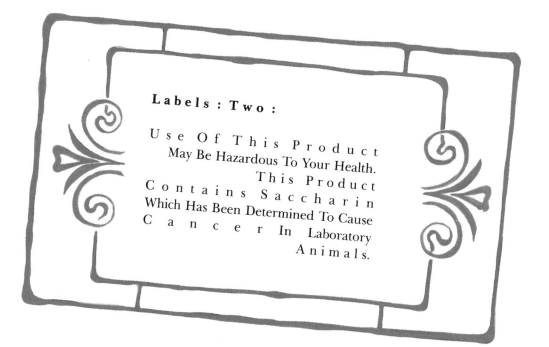

**L a b e l s : T w o :**

U s e  O f  T h i s  P r o d u c t May Be Hazardous To Your Health. T h i s  P r o d u c t C o n t a i n s  S a c c h a r i n Which Has Been Determined To Cause C a n c e r  In  Laboratory A n i m a l s.

**L a b e l s : T h r e e :**

Artificially     Sweetened     Chocolate

Artificial                   And

Marshmallow  Flavor.

**L a b e l s : F o u r :**

Instant Nonfat Dry Milk, Dairy Whey Solids,
Cocoa, Artificial Flavor, Xanthan Gum, 0.16%,
S o d i u m  S a c c h a r i n (Contains
3.2Mg.

S a c c h a r i n  P e r  O u n c e).

**L a b e l s : F i v e :**

A l l  N a t u r a l  U n
S w e e t e n e d
C h o c o l a t e.

## Rescue Mission.

One
last
lost
o n e  has  been  left, lying
twisted into the bottom
                    corner
of this otherwise empty bag,
after my fast hands have
                    done
their good work. It deserves
to rejoin the other members
of its smooth and shining
                    family.
A ride between my  r i g h t
              t h u m b
and forefinger  will  carry
                       it
                       to
pale red sisters,
brown
brothers, sweet  p a r e nts.

**The World Is In Chaos. The World Is In Flames.**

We cannot possibly remember the names of all the bad guys running around this unhappy place with bullets bombs and v a n illa frosting. When I get blue, when I get sad, when I miss the best gal I ever had, I turn inward to the rock of my unshakable faith: the belief that there must be some higher power, some gr e at cosmic and universal and timeless force far beyond my limited ability to com pre hend.

These glorious multicolor-covered chocolate c a n d i e s can really m e l t my mind.

**Facing P e n n s y l v a n i a.**

You do not notice us at airports
or single us out of the ordinary
flow of pedestrian  traffic  on
busy city streets, but  t h r e e
times each day we stop  our work
and quietly unroll  our  prayer
rugs
and kneel to face  the place  of
our glorious goddess of goodness,
our  s p i r i t u a l  home: that
far factory from which our chocolate
bars emerge to  j o u r n e y  to
our  c h o c o l a t e  s o u l s.

# SHE BAR

**Her**
**She**
**Bar**

Far
Star
I
See
You
Shining
Brown
In
My
Dark
And
Hungry
Sky

I
Wink
Back
Once
And
Fly
To
Meet
Your
Melt

**I Love My Mom  I Love My Pop.**
**I Love My Dog.   I Love My Sheep.**

But there are these candies: neatly, sweetly
stacked in four rows in each cherryred box.
They look like brown domes, like roundtop
pot tops, like flatbottomed spheres. And it
                                         is
the round top of each candy that you must
                                       bite
                                        off
to  be  able to fit the tip of your tongue
into the center  of each  one. You c a n
begin to  lick up the  creamywhite,  cherry-
flavored, sweeter-than-anything-inside-any-
thing
l i q u i d  i n  side.

At last, there is the cherry  left alone in
                                        its
chocolate candy shell. Do you pop that
whole remaining delight  i n t o
                        y o u r  mouth:
cherry
         and
chocolate together in a kind of cherrycup
you chew? Or do you  lightly  tap out the
cherry from its sweet cup  and chew it
                                       all
alone, followed by a slow slide of
chocolate cup up into your mouth?
You  can  hold  its  slowly disappearing
shape  so  lightly  between  your  tongue
and  the  roof  of  your  mouth  until it
has  gone  on  its  final  slide   down   your
                      t  h  r  o  a  t.

Oh:
I love my mom.  I love my pop.
I love my dog.    I love my sheep.
But there are these candies, and there
are boxes to go  before
                 I
                 s l e e p.

## Chocolate Dreams. Three.

I Am A Secret Scientist.
After Every One Is Fast
Asleep I Wave My Magic
Brown Candy Bar Over My
Yellow Metals And Green
Papers And Turn Gold
                                    In
                                    To
Precious
                    C h o c o l a t e.

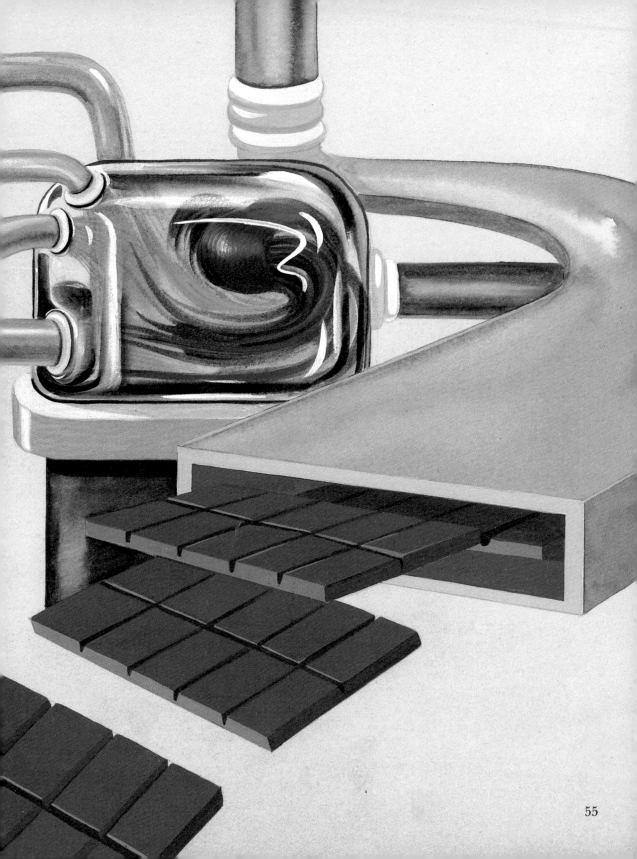

### Chocolate Dreams. Four.

Four
Teen
Tea Spoons
Per  Glass
Is A Good  Way To  Start:
Starting  Bold:  Chocolate
Syrup Luxuriously Ladled
Into      My
Darken  ing
Richen  ing
Sweetening
Swirlening
Foamen ing
Friendenly
SoHappyAnd
SmilingBackAtMe      Cold
                            Milk.

**Chocolate Dreams. Five.**

Lock Yourself In The Kitchen
On A Raining Afternoon With
All The Ingredients For Making
Chocolate Chip Cookies. First:
Open the Bag Of Chocolate
                    Chips
And
Proceed To Eat
Every One Of Them.
                Then
Mix And Bake The
Remaining
Ingredients Per Instructions.

After They Cool
You May Serve Chocolate Chipless
                Chocolate Chip
                        Cookies.

## Chocolate Dreams. Six-Thirty.


Six-Thirty, As Usual. And I Am So Sleepy
This Friday Morning. I Have To Make My Way
Into The Shower  Before School.  I Always
Notice Three Distinct Kinds Of   Air In The
Shower  Each Morning. There Is The Thick
Steam  From  The   Hot  Water. There   Is   The
Cooler Bottom Air Coming In  From  Under
The Door.  And  There  Is  The  Hot  Chocolate
                                             Air
Sliding In Through The Keyhole, Slipping
Around The Hinges, Curling  Up Through The
Floorboards From The Kitchen Down Below.
As The Water Streams Over My Face  I Close
My Eyes  And Become  A Warm Young Marsh
                                        Mallow,
Floating In A Mug  Of Brown Liquid.
I Am The Marshmallow. I Am The Mug. I Am
The Steam. I Am The Smell. I  Am  Air  And
I  Am  Liquid. I Am Odor And I Am Taste.
I Swallow Myself And Warm My Own Belly. I
Take Deep Breaths And Clear This End-Of-
Night's Foggy Dream Remains. I Clear My
Throat, I Float Awake  Into  The  Clean
And  Hungry  School  Time  Morning  Air.
I
Walk Out Of The Shower Into The  N e x t
                                  M o m e n t.

**CHOCO CHEERS.**

GIM ME  A  C
GIM ME  A  H
GIM ME  A  O
GIM ME  A  NOTHER
            C
GIM ME  A  NOTHER
            O
GIM ME  A  L
GIM ME  A  A
GIM ME  A  T
GIM ME  A  E

WAT  TA  YA  GOT
WAT  TA  YA  GOT
WAT  TA
      YA
GOT

CHONOTHERCNOTHEROLATE
CHO NOTHERC NOTHERO LATE
C H O NOTHER C NOTHER O L A T E

GO
GO
GO

62

63

# Arnold Adoff

believes that "writing a poem is making music with words and space." He is the recipient of the 1988 National Council of Teachers of English Award for Excellence in Poetry for Children, an award given every three years in recognition of a poet's body of work for young children. The announcement of the award says Adoff's poetry "is rich in quality and variety of form and topic, and speaks to children of all ages and ethnic groups."

Adoff lectures widely to children and adults and has worked with children on writing poetry in classrooms. He was born and educated in New York City and lives with his wife, the author Virginia Hamilton, in Yellow Springs, Ohio. Among his other books of poetry are *All the Colors of the Race*, *Eats*, and *Greens*.

# Turi MacCombie

was born in Troy, New York. She studied at the Emma Willard School and the Syracuse University School of Art. She says she "began drawing at age nine with the single-minded goal to become an artist." She spends her free time painting large watercolors. *Chocolate Dreams* is her first book published by Lothrop. She lives in New York City with her husband, Bruce MacCombie.